INFLATION

What it is and
How it Can be Controlled

INTRODUCTION

Price increases, or inflation, can be thought of as the gradual loss of purchasing power. The average price increase of a selection of products and services over time can serve as a proxy for the rate at which buying power declines. A unit of currency effectively buys less as a result of the increase in pricing, which is sometimes stated as a percentage. Deflation, which happens when prices fall and buying power rises, can be compared to inflation.

Human requirements go beyond simply one or two things, even if it is simple to track price changes over time for certain products. For a comfortable life, people require a wide variety of items as well as a variety of services. Commodities like food grains, metal, and fuel are among them, as are utilities like power and transportation, as well as services like labor, entertainment, and health care.

8.3%

The change in the Consumer Price Index for All Urban Consumers (CPI-U) over the 12-month period ending August 2022. When you factor out food and energy, the index rose 0.6% compared to an increase of 0.3% in July over a 12-month period. As prices grow, fewer goods and services may be purchased with a given amount of money. The general public's cost of living is affected by this loss of purchasing power, which ultimately slows economic growth. According to economists' general understanding, prolonged inflation happens when a country's money supply expands faster than its economy.

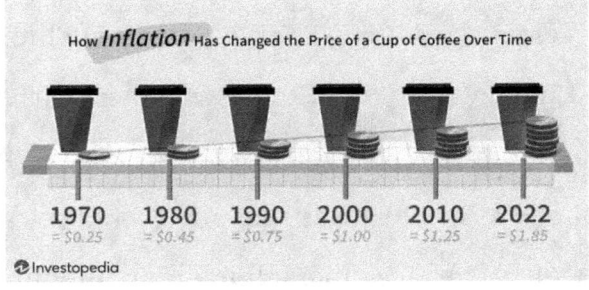

According to the Oxford English Dictionary, the phrase first used in 1838 in reference to a currency inflation and comes from the Latin inflare (to blow up or inflate) (1989).

In the years that followed, up to 1874, it was also applied to lending and price inflation. This definition of the word appears to have been strengthened when the greenback, a government-issued paper currency that quickly lost some of its value, supplanted the gold dollar during the American Civil War (1861-65).

The term inflation appeared in America in the mid-nineteenth century, "not in reference to something that happens to prices, but as something that happens to a paper currency". Today, however, it is understood as referring to a sustained increase in the general price level (as distinct from short-term fluctuations).

Other economic terms associated with inflation include deflation, which is a drop in the general level of prices, disinflation, which is a slowing of inflation, hyperinfla-

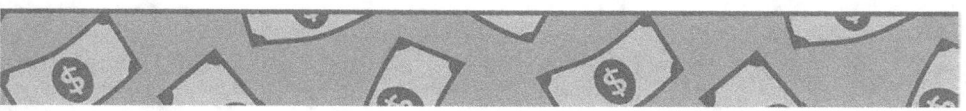

tion, stagflation, which is a combination of inflation, slow economic growth, and high unemployment, and asset price inflation, which is a general increase in the prices of financial assets without regard to their underlying value.

More specific forms of inflation refer to sectors whose prices vary semi-independently from the general trend. "House price inflation" applies to changes in the house price index while "energy inflation" is dominated by the costs of oil and gas.

By the nineteenth century, economists distinguished between three distinct factors that affect the price of goods: changes in the good's value or production costs; changes in the price of money, which at the time was typically a fluctuation in the commodity price of the metallic content in the currency; and currency depreciation due to an increase in the supply of money relative to the amount of redeemable metal backing the currency. The term "inflation" first appeared as a direct reference to the currency

depreciation that happened as the amount of redeemable banknotes exceeded the quantity of metal available for their redemption during the development of private banknote currency created during the American Civil War.

Lax monetary policy often leads to prolonged periods of high inflation. The unit value of the currency decreases, which means that its purchasing power decreases and prices increase, if the money supply increases excessively in comparison to the size of an economy. One of the first economic theories is known as the quantity theory of money, and it describes the connection between the money supply and the size of the economy.

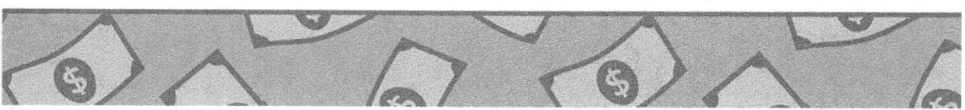

By the nineteenth century, economists distinguished between three distinct factors that affect the price of goods: changes in the good's value or production costs; changes in the price of money, which at the time was typically a fluctuation in the commodity price of the metallic content in the currency; and currency depreciation due to an increase in the supply of money relative to the amount of redeemable metal backing the currency. The term "inflation" first appeared as a direct reference to the currency depreciation that happened as the amount of redeemable banknotes exceeded the quantity of metal available for their redemption during the development of private banknote currency created during the American Civil War.

HISTORY

The existence of money, an unforeseen social construct that emerged over a period of perhaps 2500 years as a result of numerous breakthroughs and improvements, is a prerequisite for inflation. It peaked with the introduction of currency in China around 630 BC, as well as in Lydia and Ionia at the same time. As a result, inflation cannot be older than money. Periods of inflation and deflation have historically alternated while commodity money was in use, depending on the state of the economy. However, when significant quantities of gold or silver are continuously injected into an economy, this may result in protracted periods of inflation. Since the 18th century, several nations have used fiat money, allowing for far greater changes in the money supply. Politically unstable nations have experienced rapid

expansions of the money supply numerous times, leading to hyperinflations—periods of extremely high inflation rates that were substantially higher than those seen during earlier periods of commodity money. One famous instance is the hyperinflation that occurred in the German Weimar Republic. As of October 2018, Venezuela's hyperinflation was the worst in the world, with an annual inflation rate of 833,997%. From the price revolution of the 16th century, which was fueled by the influx of gold and particularly silver that the Spaniards seized and mined in Latin America, to the largest paper money inflation of all time in Hungary after World War II, there have been inflations of varying sizes throughout history. Under contrast, inflation has been kept in check and stable in nations with independent central banks since the 1980s. The result has been what is known as the "Great Moderation," a slowing of the business cycle and less variance in major macroeconomic indices.

Historical inflationary periods

Throughout history, many different civilizations have experienced abrupt increases in the amount of money or in the total amount of money available, altering as new types of

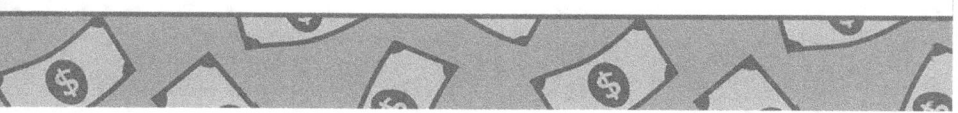

Fineness of early Roman imperial silver coins

money were introduced. When silver was used as money, for instance, the government might gather silver coins, melt them down, mix them with other metals like copper or lead, and then reissue them at the same nominal value. This process is known as debasement. The denarius held more than 90% silver when Nero became emperor of Rome in AD 54, but by the 270s, there was almost no silver remaining. The government may produce more coins without using more silver by mixing other metals into the silver to dilute it.

Ancient China

China during the Song Dynasty is where the custom of printing paper money to generate fiat currency first emerged. The government of the Mongol Yuan Dynasty spent a lot of money on expensive battles and then responded by printing additional money, which caused inflation. The Ming Period first rejected the use of paper money and returned to the usage of copper coins out of fear of the inflation that afflicted the Yuan dynasty.

Medieval Egypt

According to legend, a camel train with thousands of people and close to a hundred camels followed the Malian monarch Mansa Musa on his hajj to Mecca in 1324. He spent or gave away so much gold when he was in Cairo that it lowered the price and decreased the purchasing power of gold in Egypt for more than a decade. A modern Arab historian said the following concerning Mansa Musa's visit:

"Gold was at a high price in Egypt until they came in that year. The mithqal did not go below 25 dirhams and was generally above, but from that time its value fell and it cheapened in price and has remained cheap till now. The mithqal does not exceed 22 dirhams or less. This has been the state of affairs for about twelve years until this day by reason of the large amount of gold which they brought into Egypt and spent there."

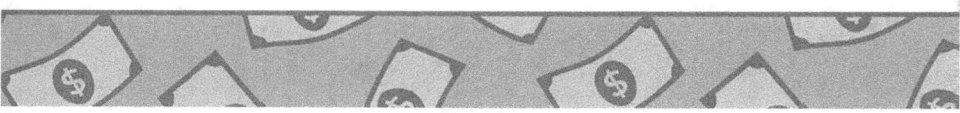

From the second half of the 15th century to the first half of the 17th, Western Europe experienced a major inflationary cycle referred to as the "price revolution", with prices on average rising perhaps sixfold over 150 years. This is often attributed to the influx of gold and silver from the New World into Habsburg Spain, with wider availability of silver in previously cash-starved Europe causing widespread inflation. European population rebound from the Black Death began before the arrival of New World metal, and may have began a process of inflation that New World silver compounded later in the 16th century.

MEASURES

Given that there are many possible measures of the price level, there are many possible measures of price inflation. Most frequently, the term "inflation" refers to a rise in a broad price index representing the overall price level for goods and services in the economy. The Consumer Price Index (CPI), the Personal consumption expenditures price index (PCEPI) and the GDP deflator are some examples of broad price indices. However, "inflation" may also be used to describe a rising price level within a narrower set of assets, goods or services within the economy, such as commodities (including food, fuel, metals), tangible assets (such as real estate), financial assets (such as stocks, bonds), services (such as entertainment and health care), or labor.

Although the values of capital assets are often casually said to "inflate," this should not be confused with inflation as a defined term; a more accurate description for an increase in the value of a capital asset is appreciation. The FBI (CCI), the Producer Price Index, and Employment Cost Index (ECI) are examples of narrow price indices used to measure price inflation in particular sectors of the economy. Core inflation is a measure of inflation for a subset of consumer prices that excludes food and energy prices, which rise and fall more than other prices in the short term. The Federal Reserve Board pays particular attention to the core inflation rate to get a better estimate of long-term future inflation trends overall. The inflation rate is most widely calculated by determining the movement or change in a price index, typically the consumer price index.[39] The inflation rate is the percentage change of a price index over time. The Retail Prices Index is also a measure of inflation that is commonly used in the United Kingdom. It is broader than the

CPI and contains a larger basket of goods and services. Given the recent high inflation, the RPI is indicative of the experiences of a wide range of household types, particularly low-income households.

To illustrate the method of calculation, in January 2007, the U.S. Consumer Price Index was 202.416, and in January 2008 it was 211.080. The formula for calculating the annual percentage rate inflation in the CPI over the course of the year is:

$$\left(\frac{211.080 - 202.416}{202.416}\right) \times 100\% = 4.28\%$$

The resulting inflation rate for the CPI in this one-year period is 4.28%, meaning the general level of prices for typical U.S. consumers rose by approximately four percent in 2007.

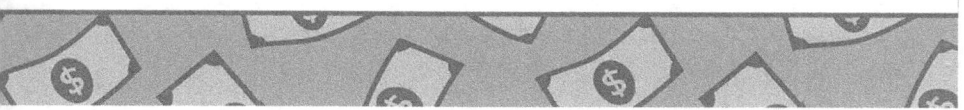

Other widely used price indices for calculating price inflation include the following:

Producer Price Indices (PPIs): which measures average changes in prices received by domestic producers for their output. This differs from the CPI in that price subsidization, profits, and taxes may cause the amount received by the producer to differ from what the consumer paid. There is also typically a delay between an increase in the PPI and any eventual increase in the CPI. Producer price index measures the pressure being put on producers by the costs of their raw materials. This could be "passed on" to consumers, or it could be absorbed by profits, or offset by increasing productivity. In India and the United States, an earlier version of the PPI was called the Wholesale price index.

Commodity Price Indices: which measure the price of a selection of commodities. In the present commodity price indices are weighted by the relative importance of the components to the "all in" cost of an employee.

Core Price Indices: because food and oil prices can change quickly due to changes in supply and demand conditions in the food and oil markets, it can be difficult to detect the long run trend in price levels when those prices are included. Therefore, most statistical agencies also report a measure of 'core inflation', which removes the most volatile components (such as food and oil) from a broad price index like the CPI. Because core inflation is less affected by short run supply and demand conditions in specific markets, central banks rely on it to better measure the inflationary effect of current monetary policy.

Other common measures of inflation are:

GDP deflator is a measure of the price of all the goods and services included in gross domestic product (GDP). The US Commerce Department publishes a deflator series for US GDP, defined as its nominal GDP measure divided by its real GDP measure.

Regional Inflation: The Bureau of Labor Statistics breaks down CPI-U calculations down to different regions of the US.

Historical Inflation: Before collecting consistent econometric data became standard for governments, and for the purpose of comparing absolute, rather than relative standards of living, various economists have calculated imputed inflation figures. Most inflation data before the early 20th century is imputed based on the known costs of goods, rather than compiled at the time. It is also used to adjust for the differences in real standard of living for the presence of technology.

Asset price Inflation: is an undue increase in the prices of real or financial assets, such as stock (equity) and real estate. While there is no widely accepted index of this type, some central bankers have suggested that it would be better to aim at stabilizing a wider general price level inflation measure that includes some asset prices, instead of stabilizing CPI or core in-

flation only. The reason is that by raising interest rates when stock prices or real estate prices rise, and lowering them when these asset prices fall, central banks might be more successful in avoiding bubbles and crashes in asset prices.

Issues in measuring

A common set of commodities and services must have their nominal prices changed in order to measure inflation in an economy. These price changes must be distinguished from those caused by changes in value, such as changes in volume, quality, or performance. For instance, if the cost of a can of corn rises from $0.90 to $1.00 in the span of a year without a change in quality, this price difference is an example of inflation. However, this one-time price change wouldn't be indicative of typical inflation in the economy as a whole. The price change of a sizable "basket" of representative goods and services is calculated in order to calculate total inflation. This is what a price index, which is the total cost of a "basket" of various goods and services, is intended to do.

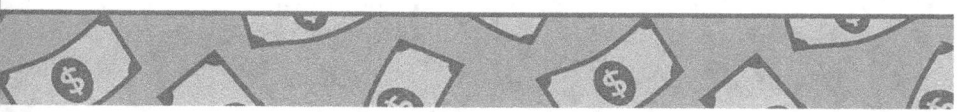

The weighted average price of the goods in the "basket" is what makes up the total price. The unit price of an item is multiplied by the quantity that the typical consumer purchases to arrive at a weighted pricing. Weighted pricing is a crucial tool for determining how individual unit price increases affect overall inflation in the economy. For instance, the Consumer Price Index analyzes information gathered from household surveys to establish what percentage of the average consumer's overall spending is spent on particular goods and services, and then weights the average prices of those items. The total price is determined by adding those weighted average values. Indexes often select a price from the "base year" and give it a value of 100 to better reflect price fluctuations over time. Then, index prices in succeeding years are stated in relation to the price of the base year. One must also consider the base effect when comparing inflation measures across time periods.

The relative weight of the items in the basket or how current goods and services are compared to earlier goods and services are two common ways that inflation estimates change through time. To reflect changes in customer behavior, basket weights are changed frequently, typically once a year. A weighting bias in the assessment of inflation can still be introduced by abrupt changes in consumer behavior. For instance, it has been demonstrated that during the COVID-19 pandemic, the basket of goods and services was no longer a true reflection of consumption because many of these items could no longer be consumed due to government containment measures (also known as "lock-downs").

Over time, adjustments are also made to the type of goods and services selected to reflect changes in the sorts of goods and services purchased by 'typical consumers'. New products may be introduced, older products disappear, the quality of existing products may

change, and consumer preferences can shift. Both the sorts of goods and services which are included in the "basket" and the weighted price used in inflation measures will be changed over time to keep pace with the changing marketplace.[citation needed] Different segments of the population may naturally consume different "baskets" of goods and services and may even experience different inflation rates. It is argued that companies have put more innovation into bringing down prices for wealthy families than for poor families.

Inflation numbers are often seasonally adjusted to differentiate expected cyclical cost shifts. For example, home heating costs are expected to rise in colder months, and seasonal adjustments are often used when measuring for inflation to compensate

When looking at inflation, economic institutions may focus only on certain kinds of prices, or special indices, such as the core inflation index which is used by central banks to formulate monetary policy.

Most inflation indices are calculated from weighted averages of selected price changes. This necessarily introduces distortion, and can lead to legitimate disputes about what the true inflation rate is. This problem can be overcome by including all available price changes in the calculation, and then choosing the median value. In some other cases, governments may intentionally report false inflation rates; for instance, during the presidency of Cristina Kirchner (2007–2015) the government of Argentina was criticised for manipulating economic data, such as inflation and GDP figures, for political gain and to reduce payments on its inflation-indexed debt.

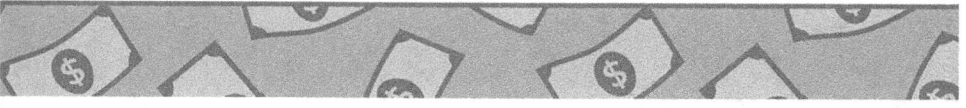

Inflation expectations

Inflation expectations or expected inflation is the rate of inflation that is anticipated for some period of time in the foreseeable future. There are two major approaches to modeling the formation of inflation expectations. Adaptive expectations models them as a weighted average of what was expected one period earlier and the actual rate of inflation that most recently occurred. Rational expectations models them as unbiased, in the sense that the expected inflation rate is not systematically above or systematically below the inflation rate that actually occurs.

The University of Michigan poll has been a reliable source of inflation expectations data for many years. The economy is impacted by inflation expectations in a number of ways. They are essentially incorporated into nominal interest rates, thus a change in predicted inflation will often cause a change in nominal interest rates as well, with little to no impact on real interest rates.

Additionally, increased predicted inflation often gets included into the pace of salary increases, meaning that changes in real earnings have less of an impact, if any at all. Additionally, how inflationary expectations react to monetary policy can affect how the consequences of policy are distributed between inflation and unemployment.

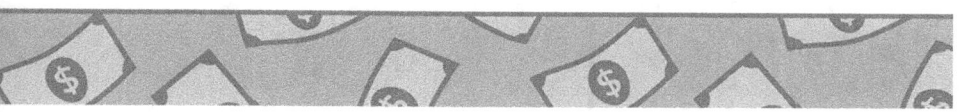

MONETARIST VIEW

The rate at which the money supply expands or contracts, according to monetarists, is the primary factor affecting whether there is inflation or deflation. They believe that government spending and taxes, or fiscal policy, are inefficient at containing inflation. Milton Friedman, a monetarist economist, is credited with saying that "inflation is always and everywhere a monetary phenomena."

Monetarists assert that the empirical study of monetary history shows that inflation has always been a monetary phenomenon. The quantity theory of money, simply stated, says that any change in the amount of money in a system will change the price level. This theory begins with the equation of exchange:

Additionally, increased predicted inflation often gets included into the pace of salary increases, meaning that changes in real earnings have less of an impact, if any at all. Additionally, how inflationary expectations react to monetary policy can affect how the consequences of policy are distributed between inflation and unemployment.

$MV=PQ$

where

M is the nominal quantity of money;

V is the velocity of money in final expenditures;

P is the general price level;

Q is an index of the real value of final expenditures;

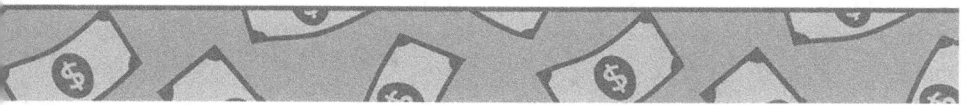

Monetarists believe that the productive capacity of the economy determines the actual value of production over the long term and that monetary policy has no effect on the velocity of money (at least in the long run). According to these hypotheses, changes in the amount of money are the main cause of the change in the overall price level. The money supply affects the value of nominal production (which equals final expenditure) in the short run when exogenous velocity (i.e., velocity set externally and unaffected by monetary policy) prevails.

In practice, velocity is not exogenous in the short run, and so the formula does not necessarily imply a stable short-run relationship between the money supply and nominal output. However, in the long run, changes in velocity are assumed to be determined by the evolution of the payments mechanism. If velocity is relatively unaffected by monetary policy, the long-run rate of increase in prices (the inflation rate) is equal to the long-run

of increase in prices (the inflation rate) is equal to the long-run growth rate of the money supply plus the exogenous long-run rate of velocity growth minus the long.

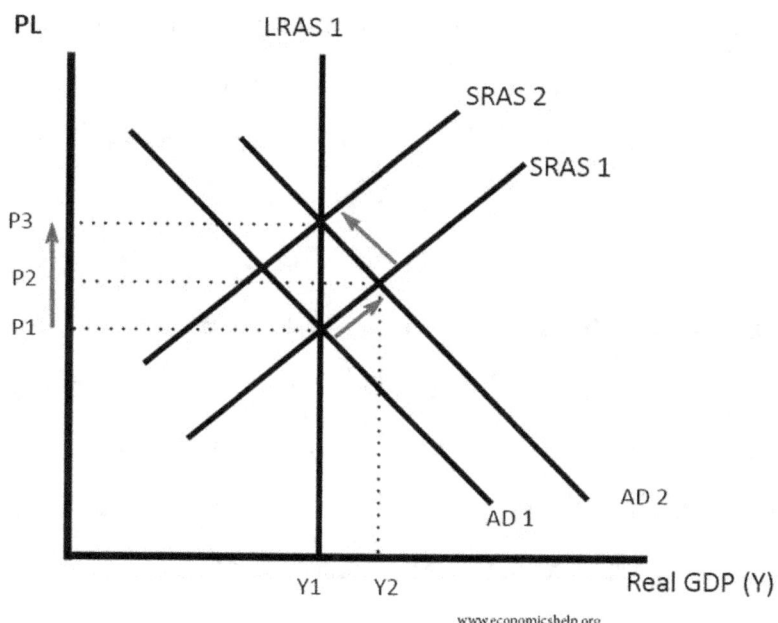

KEYNESIAN VIEW

Keynesian economics proposes that changes in the money supply do not directly affect prices in the short run, and that visible inflation is the result of demand pressures in the economy expressing themselves in prices.

There are three major sources of inflation, as part of what Robert J. Gordon calls the "triangle model":

Demand-pull inflation: is brought on by increases in aggregate demand as a result of rising private and public spending, among other things. Demand inflation promotes economic growth since it will spur investment and expansion due to the excess demand and favorable market circumstances.

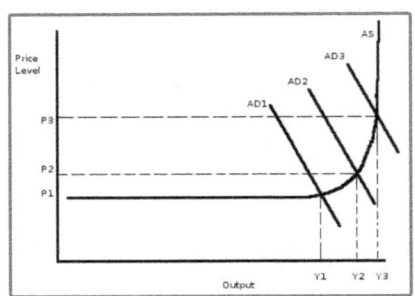

Cost-push inflation: sometimes known as "supply shock inflation," is brought on by a decrease in overall supply (potential output). This might be a result of conflict, natural calamities, or rising input costs. Cost-push inflation, for instance, can result from a sudden drop in oil supply that raises oil prices. The expense of oil to producers might then be passed on to consumers in the form of higher pricing. Another illustration comes from unexpectedly high insured losses, whether they were caused by real catastrophes or fake ones (which might be particularly prevalent in times of recession). Employees may seek quick wage increases in order to stay up with consumer prices in an environment of high inflation. According to the cost-push inflation theory, increasing wages themselves can

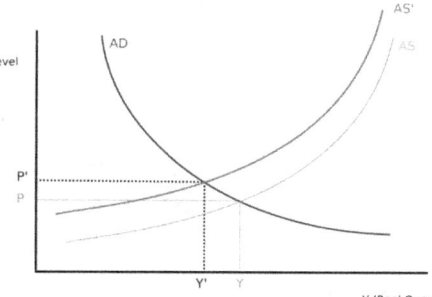

Built-in inflation: is induced by adaptive expectations, and is often linked to the "price/wage spiral". It involves workers trying to keep their wages up with prices (above the rate of inflation), and firms passing these higher labor costs on to their customers as higher prices, leading to a feedback loop. Built-in inflation reflects events in the past, and so might be seen as hangover inflation.

EFFECTS OF INFLATION

General effect: The loss of a currency's purchasing power is referred to as inflation. In other words, each unit of currency can buy less overall goods and services as prices grow. Different economic sectors are affected differently by inflation, with some experiencing negative effects and others experiencing positive effects. For instance, when there is inflation, individuals in society who own physical assets such as real estate, stocks, etc. benefit from an increase in the price or worth of their holdings, but those who want to buy them will have to pay more. The extent to which their income is set will determine their ability to do so. Also, individuals or institutions with cash assets will experience a decline in the purchasing power of the cash.

Increases in the price level (inflation) erode the real value of money (the functional currency) and other items with an underlying monetary nature.

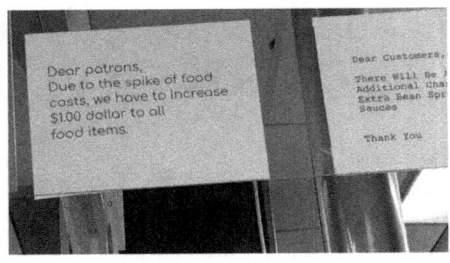

The "actual" interest rate will decrease for borrowers who have obligations with fixed nominal interest rates as the inflation rate increases. The nominal interest rate less the inflation rate equals the real interest on a loan. As long as both the nominal interest rate and the inflation rate are low, the formula R = N-I comes close to giving the right answer. The proper formula is r = n/i, where r, n, and I are ratios (for example, 1.2 for +20%, 0.8 for 20%). For instance, a loan with a nominal interest rate of 5% and an inflation rate of 3% would have a real interest rate of roughly 2% (it is actually 1.94%).

NEGATIVE

High or erratic inflation rates are thought to be detrimental to the health of the economy as a whole. They increase market inefficiencies and make it challenging for businesses to manage long-term budgets. As businesses are compelled to divert resources away from products and services in order to concentrate on profit and losses from currency inflation, inflation can be a drag on productivity. Investment and saving are discouraged when there is uncertainty regarding the future buying value of money. Hidden tax hikes may also be imposed via inflation. For instance, unless the tax brackets are updated to inflation, inflated earnings force taxpayers into higher income tax rates.

Hoarding

In order to protect their riches against predicted losses due to the diminishing purchasing power of money, which would result in shortages of the hoarded products, people purchase durable and/or non-perishable commodities as well as other things.

Social unrest and revolts

Large-scale protests and revolutions may result from inflation. For instance, many analysts, including Robert Zoellick, president of the World Bank, believe that inflation, particularly food inflation, was a major factor in both the 2011 Egyptian Revolution and the 2010–2011 Tunisian Revolution. After only 18 days of protests, both Egyptian President Hosni Mubarak and Tunisian President Zine El Abidine Ben Ali were overthrown, and demonstrations quickly extended to numerous other nations in North Africa and the Middle East.any countries of North Africa and Middle East.

Hyperinflation

If inflation becomes too high, it can cause people to severely curtail their use of the currency, leading to an acceleration in the inflation rate. High and accelerating inflation grossly interferes with the normal workings of the economy, hurting its ability to supply goods. Hyperinflation can lead people to abandon the use of the country's currency in

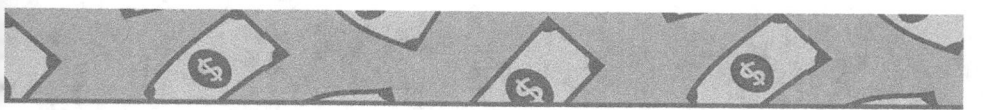

Allocative efficiency

A change in the supply or demand for a good will normally cause its relative price to change, signaling the buyers and sellers that they should re-allocate resources in response to the new market conditions. But when prices are constantly changing due to inflation, price changes due to genuine relative price signals are difficult to distinguish from price changes due to general inflation, so agents are slow to respond to them. The result is a loss of allocative efficiency.

Shoe leather cost

High inflation makes holding cash balances more costly and may lead consumers to keep more of their assets in interest-bearing accounts. But because transactions still require currency, more "trips to the bank" are required to make withdrawals, figuratively wearing out the "shoe leather" with each journey.

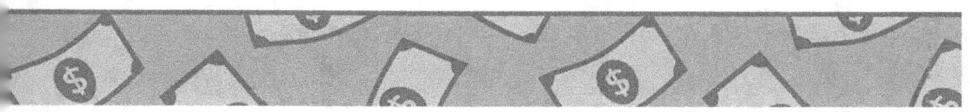

POSITIVE

Labour-market adjustments

The nominal salary is sluggish to decrease. Long-term disequilibrium and excessive unemployment on the labor market may result from this. Moderate inflation speeds up the process of labor markets reaching equilibrium because it permits real wages to decline even while nominal wages are held constant.

Room to maneuver

The primary tools for controlling the money supply are the ability to set the discount rate, the rate at which banks can borrow from the central bank, and open market operations, which are the central bank's interventions into the bonds market with the aim of affecting the nominal interest rate. If an economy finds itself in a recession with already low, or even zero, nominal interest rates, then the bank cannot cut these rates further (since negative nominal interest rates are impossible) to stimulate the economy – this situation is known as a liquidity trap.

The Nobel laureate Robert Mundell noticed that moderate inflation would drive savers to substitute lending for some money holding as a means of financing future expenditure. This relationship between inflation and capital investment is known as the Mundell-Tobin effect. Real interest rates for market clearing would decrease as a result of that substitution. The lower real rate of interest would encourage more borrowing to fund investments. In a similar vein, Nobel laureate James Tobin remarked that such inflation would force businesses to forego investing in cash balances in their asset portfolios in favor of investments in physical capital (plant, equipment, and inventory). That substitution would mean choosing the making of investments with lower rates of real return. (The rates of return are lower because the investments with higher rates of return were already being made before.) The two related effects are known as the Mundell–Tobin effect.

Instability with deflation

Economist S.C. Tsiang noted that once substantial deflation is expected, two important effects will appear; both a result of money holding substituting for lending as a vehicle for saving. The first was that continually falling prices and the resulting incentive to hoard money will cause instability resulting from the likely increasing fear, while money hoards grow in value, that the value of those hoards are at risk, as people realize that a movement to trade those money hoards for real goods and assets will quickly drive those prices up. Any movement to spend those hoards "once started would become a tremendous avalanche, which could rampage for a long time before it would spend itself." Thus, a regime of long-term deflation is likely to be interrupted by periodic spikes of rapid inflation and consequent real economic disruptions. The second effect noted by Tsiang is that when savers have substituted money holding for lending on financial markets, the role of those markets in channeling sav-

ings into investment is undermined. With nominal interest rates driven to zero, or near zero, from the competition with a high return money asset, there would be no price mechanism in whatever is left of those markets. With financial markets effectively euthanized, the remaining goods and physical asset prices would move in perverse directions. For example, an increased desire to save could not push interest rates further down (and thereby stimulate investment) but would instead cause additional money hoarding, driving consumer prices further down and making investment in consumer goods production thereby less attractive. Moderate inflation, once its expectation is incorporated into nominal interest rates, would give those interest rates room to go both up and down in response to shifting investment opportunities, or savers' preferences, and thus allow financial markets to function in a more normal fashion.

CONTROLLING INFLATION

Monetary policy

Monetary policy is the policy enacted by the monetary authorities (most frequently the central bank of a nation) to control the interest rate – or equivalently the money supply – so as to control inflation and ensure price stability. Higher interest rates reduce the economy's money supply because fewer people seek loans. When banks make loans, the loan proceeds are generally deposited in bank accounts that are part of the money supply, thereby expanding it. When banks make fewer loans, the amount of bank deposits and hence the money supply decrease. For example, in the early 1980s, when the US federal funds rate exceeded 15%, the quantity of Federal Reserve dollars fell 8.1%, from US$8.6 trillion down to $7.9 trillion.

In the latter half of the 20th century, there was debate between Keynesians and monetarists about the appropriate instrument to use to control inflation. Monetar-

ists emphasize a low and steady growth rate of the money supply, while Keynesians emphasize controlling aggregate demand, by reducing demand during economic expansions and increasing demand during recessions to keep inflation stable. Control of aggregate demand can be achieved by using either monetary policy or fiscal policy (increasing taxation or reducing government spending to reduce demand). Ever since the 1980s, most countries have primarily relied on monetary policy to control inflation. When inflation beyond an acceptable level takes place, the country's central bank increases the interest rate, which will tend to slow down economic growth and inflation. Some central banks have a symmetrical inflation target, while others only react when inflation rises above a certain threshold.

In the 21st century, most economists favor a low and steady rate of inflation. In most countries, central banks or other monetary authorities are tasked with keeping interest rates and prices stable. and inflation near a target rate. These inflation targets may be pub-

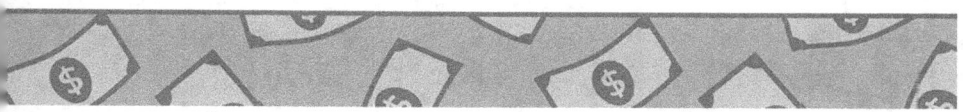

licly disclosed or not. In most OECD countries, the inflation target is usually about 2% to 3%. Central banks target a low inflation rate because they believe that high inflation is economically costly because it would create uncertainty about differences in relative prices and about the inflation rate itself. A low positive inflation rate is targeted rather than a zero or negative one because the latter could cause or worsen recessions; low (as opposed to zero or negative) inflation reduces the severity of economic recessions by enabling the labor market to adjust more quickly in a downturn, and reduces the risk that a liquidity trap prevents monetary policy from stabilizing the economy.

Other methods

FIXED EXCHANGE RATE

A region's primary means of trade under the gold standard is paper money (or another type of currency token) that is often freely convertible into predetermined, fixed amounts of gold. The standard details the implementation of the gold backing, including the amount of specie per unit of money. Although the currency itself has no intrinsic worth, dealers accept it since it can be exchanged for the corresponding amount of specie. For instance, a U.S. silver certificate could be exchanged for a real silver coin.

Under the Bretton Woods agreement, most countries around the world had currencies that were fixed to the U.S. dollar. This limited inflation in those countries, but also exposed them to the danger of speculative attacks. After the Bretton Woods agreement broke down in the early 1970s, countries gradually turned to floating exchange rates. However, in the later part of the 20th century, some countries reverted to a fixed exchange rate as part of an attempt to control inflation. This policy of using a fixed exchange rate to control inflation was used in many countries in South America in the later part of the 20th century (e.g. Argentina (1991–2002), Bolivia, Brazil, Chile, Pakistan, etc.).

GOLD STANDARD

A region's primary means of trade under the gold standard is paper money (or another type of currency token) that is often freely convertible into predetermined, fixed amounts of gold. The standard details the implementation of the gold backing, including the amount of specie per unit of money. Although the currency itself has no intrinsic worth, dealers accept it since it can be exchanged for the corresponding amount of specie. For instance, a U.S. silver certificate could be exchanged for a real silver coin. The gold standard was partially abandoned via the international adoption of the

Bretton Woods system. Under this system all other major currencies were tied at fixed rates to the US dollar, which itself was tied by the US government to gold at the rate of US$35 per ounce. The Bretton Woods system broke down in 1971, causing most countries to switch to fiat money – money backed only by the laws of the country.

The increasing rate of the supply of gold in relation to total output would determine the long-term rate of inflation (or deflation) under a gold standard. The inflation rate will fluctuate arbitrarily as a result, according to critics, and gold mining would virtually dictate monetary policy.

Wage and price controls

Wage and price controls are another strategy that has been tried in the past ("incomes policies"). In conjunction with rationing, wage and price limitations have been beneficial during times of war. Their application in other circumstances, however, is much more erratic. A notable example of its misuse is Richard Nixon's implementation of wage and price restrictions in 1972. The Prices and Incomes Accord in Australia and the Wassenaar Agreement in the Netherlands serve as more effective examples.

In general, wage and price controls are regarded as a temporary and exceptional measure, only effective when coupled with policies designed to reduce the underlying causes of inflation during the wage and price control regime, for example, winning the war being fought. They often have perverse effects, due to the distorted signals they send to the market. Artificially low

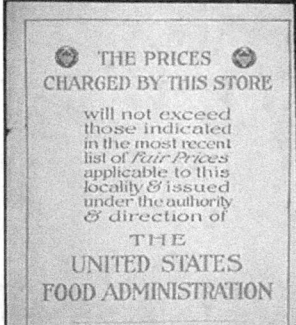

prices often cause rationing and shortages and discourage future investment, resulting in yet further shortages. The usual economic analysis is that any product or service that is under-priced is overconsumed. For example, if the official price of bread is too low, there will be too little bread at official prices, and too little investment in bread making by the market to satisfy future needs, thereby exacerbating the problem in the long term.

Temporary controls could be used in conjunction with a recession to combat inflation. This would reduce the need to raise unemployment while also preventing the kinds of distortions that temporary controls lead to when demand is high. The advise of economists is often to liberalize prices rather than implement price controls because they believe that the economy will adjust and stop engaging in unprofitable activities. Because of the decreased activity, the labor or resource prices that were fueling inflation will decline along with overall economic production. This often produces a severe recession, as productive capacity is reallocated and is thus often very unpopular with the people whose livelihoods are destroyed.

www.ingramcontent.com/pod-product-compliance
Lightning Source LLC
Chambersburg PA
CBHW050025230526
45470CB00003B/1137